THE LORD'S PRAYER

ELECT'S PRAYER GUIDE

The Holy One of Israel

CONTENTS

Chapter 1

Prayer: Overview

One of the most difficult things to do in this world is to pray. Its difficulty does not come from having a hard time getting up or dragging yourself to the Lord's presence; in fact, these are very much easy to do, as long as God is in charge. What makes prayer very difficult is the content of it; the desires and lust of the flesh often against the will of God. It is easy to get up; easy to go to Him, but it is not an easy task to pray correctly. Well, for some people, it is the opposite. Most find it difficult to get up, or dedicate their time to prayer, however, the moment they are able to do this, they find it very easy to open their mouth and begin to say something.

Prayer is difficult because it (the flesh) is hard to deal with. Particularly, when it is not done rightly, it is much easier to curse oneself through one's prayer/request. If it were not necessary, the Word would never have mentioned a guide; a template every believer is expected to model his/her prayers after.

Imagine you praying for a family member or a close friend, telling God, "God, please grant all the desires of my friend's heart". Yet, one desire which

[1]

your supposed friend has made his top priority is your downfall. Now, if God were to answer your prayer, you see it would be to your detriment. Should the downfall come, you would not know where it came from. You would think it was the devil, but no, it was not. It was you!

Oftentimes, what we want is not needed. Well, physically, it looks like we could die from not owning it, however, God knows that the very request (if granted) is at the detriment of the spirit, while the flesh is gratified. If God answered these requests then, you realize that you drift apart from God. You probably would be tricked into thinking that you draw nearer to God because your offering and tithe have increased, but little do you know that the part of you, which is most important to God, your heart, has since drifted from the way of the Creator.

When praying for individuals, and even oneself, there is need to be careful. This is why the Scripture states that we do not know what to pray for, but the Spirit helps. Know this that, the Spirit helps only when you allow it, and when He does help, He makes intercession on your behalf according to the will of God, not (according to) the desires of your flesh. Because of this, Jesus Christ gave a template, so that we do not pray amiss, or curse ourselves through our prayers. When you pray for wealth, when it is clear that it would cause your downfall, you are inadvertently cursing yourself. Tell me, what greater curse is there than eternal condemnation and everlasting torment in the lake of fire?

Prayer is an activity done out of care and fear. You could as well be plotting your own downfall through your requests to God. In the prayer guide given by the Lord, there is a very important phrase which clears all these worries and probable mistakes our mortal self is capable of making while we pray. Sadly, many leave it out. People hardly mention or include it in their prayers. Many people would rather the preacher told them "May God answer all your prayers", than hear the preacher said that particular phrase. Yet, this phrase is much more important than the entire body of your requests. While your requests might be misleading and self-destructive, this phrase acts as 'check'; taking out the unnecessary, and leaving the necessary. The statement is, "Your will be done…"

The template can generally be classified into three parts; the opening (Thanksgiving), Your requests, The closing or end (Thanksgiving). It starts with giving thanks to God, and ends with same. Also, the statement, "Your will be done…" comes before any personal request; in fact, it immediately comes after the opening thanksgiving. This is to show its importance. It goes right before the requests, so, if any of the prayers to follow does not align with God's will for one's life, the Spirit separates such from the rest of the request.

Jesus Christ says, "Seek ye first the Kingdom of God, and His righteousness…" and this is reflected in the template. Well over third of four parts of the Lord's prayer focus on "the Kingdom of God". The only material substance considered important is the daily bread (food), which is necessary to keep the body going. No part of it focuses on wealth, the destruction of one's foes, or other trivial material substance. The prayer starts with giving thanks to God, and ends with giving glory to God; which is the primary purpose of man's existence on the earth.

It is very crucial then, for anyone who does not want to pray amiss, to follow this pattern. Giving thanks, declaring that God's will be done, asking for provision, forgiveness, grace to overcome day-to-day temptation, and deliverance from evil, extension of these prayers to friends and loved ones; not leaving out one's nation, and lastly, thanksgiving. As long as one has kicked off the request by asking that God's will prevails over all others, one can go ahead to ask for anything or pray for anyone (with confidence that only the important requests which align with God's will and have no tendency of harming us in the process will be granted).

Before each classification is looked into, we shall consider three things; praying in the Spirit, Praying in tongues, and, in whose name shall we pray? Once this truth in the Father has been established, we move on to learn deeper the Lord's Prayer.

Praying in the Spirit

What does it really mean to pray in the Spirit? Consider the time of old. God instructed Moses, who would later relay to the priest, how offerings should be made. There is a vital feature which, without it, the offering would be nothing before God. It will neither be transformed nor reach up to God in heaven. This vital feature is FIRE. Indeed, without the fire, the goat or any other animal would only lie there on the altar, unrecognized by God, because what would have transformed it was missing. Specifically, God instructed that the fire must NEVER go out of the altar.

Fire is a symbol of God's Spirit. During that period, the altar was a physical space, unlike now when offerings and worship are made directly from the heart of man. When the Holy Spirit (fire) is missing in the heart of an individual then, the act of such individual is nothing before God. The prayers we say, the songs we sing, are transformed by the activities of the Holy Spirit, so these rise up to God like Aaron's incense; if the Holy Spirit is missing then, it is likened to Aaron preparing the spices but having no fire to light it up.

The act of burning incense and praying in the Spirit have the same meaning. At the time of old, burning incense would be impossible without fire. At this period, praying to God in an acceptable manner would be impossible if the Holy Spirit were absent.

God basically commanded that the fire must never go out. The fire burning in the altar must continuously burn. Similarly, the fire of God's Spirit burning in your heart must never go out. If it did for a moment, unclean spirits would sooner come creeping in, which would make it uninhabitable for God's Spirit. The fire—burning passion and zeal—must never be put out.

Praying in Spirit simply is praying to God with the Holy Spirit dwelling in you. It is the Holy Spirit who guides you on what to say or how to pray; for we cannot do any of these things on our own. Here, a clear distinction must be made between prayers said while the Spirit leads and prayers said while the flesh/emotions lead.

Oftentimes, people pray the way they are led by their flesh. When the disciples were led by flesh and emotions, they saw 'people' as the enemies. John and James desired to call down fire to wipe out a settlement because they (the people) rejected their Master. A disciple drew out a sword and cut off the ear of one in defense of his Master. However, after they had the Holy Spirit dwelling in them, and the fire actively burning, they began to see 'spirit', 'unseen forces' as the enemies; not 'people'. Paul wrote, we do not wrestle against flesh and blood, but against principalities and powers.

For someone who lives and is governed by the flesh, you think the rulers in your nation are the enemies. But for one who is led by the Spirit of God, he knows that the real struggle is between the devil and God's people; the one who pushes the physical power to make unfavourable policies is the unclean spirit working behind the scenes.

When you are led by emotions, you begin to pray for the flesh (your enemies) to die or suffer misfortune, while God blesses you, makes you wealthy, and never see persecution or trial. When you are led by the Spirit, you rebuke the unseen forces behind the decisions of the flesh (your enemies), and continually ask for grace to overcome temptations when they come. While one who is led by emotions will consistently pray for material wealth, the one who is led by the Spirit of God will say, "Lord, if I will forsake your ways as a result of my wealth, then never give me this wealth".

Many indeed say prayers which are led by emotions/flesh, and this is how many continue to miss it, because often, your flesh desires things which are destructive to your spirit. These are two extremes, both striving to own and control the soul. If you live by the flesh, it will lead your soul to a place of eternal damnation. If you live by the Spirit, He leads you to a place of peace, and eternal rest. If you live by the Spirit, then you will not fulfil the lust of the flesh.

Needless to say, every elect must pray in the Spirit at all times. Of course, having the indwelling of God's Spirit is a prerequisite for being an elect of God. And even when we pray, we must not pray like the non-elect do; they like to follow the pattern of the world, praying on the streets, and praying so loud that men may see them, and credit their level of 'spirituality'. When you pray, you lock yourself in your closet, and pray to your God in heaven. The One who is everywhere at every time then hears your secret prayers and give you a reward all eyes see.

The true worshippers worship God and pray to Him in Spirit and in Truth. Their prayers are transformed by God's Spirit who does the task of filtering out those requests we really do not need or the ones which would lay the bed for destruction.

Lastly, praying in the Spirit is done in human languages. Otherwise, would you say my Lord never prayed in the Spirit, or that the disciples never prayed in the Spirit, or the prophets never prayed in the Spirit? God is the Creator of the different languages of the world, and He is a Master of these languages. When you communicate with Him then, communicate in a language He has made. Praying in the Spirit is praying fruitfully. Pray in a language which you understand. Pray in a language in which you fully understand exactly what you are asking God for. Praying in the Spirit basically means having the indwelling of God's Spirit, which is the fire that transforms your prayers from words into the incense offering which rises up to God. When you have the indwelling of God's Spirit, He leads your prayers instead of your emotions or your flesh occupying the driving seat. Even when your flesh gets in the way, the Holy Spirit weighs your requests in the process of its transformation, taking out the excesses, and leaving only those necessary parts to go up to God.

If we do not pray in the Spirit, our flesh will often lead us astray. The flesh loves pleasure, and the ways of the world. If we let it handle the way we approach God in prayers, it will not be good for our spirit; for the flesh seeks only after those things which are of the world. The Word admonishes that we pray in the Spirit that we may not fulfil the lust of the flesh. Jesus Christ prayed in the Spirit. The apostles prayed in the Spirit. Every elect of God then must as well pray in the Spirit. Praying in the Spirit is letting the Spirit lead one in prayer, and not one's flesh. This can only be achieved if one truly has the indwelling of the Holy Spirit, and is in complete subjection to the will of the Holy Spirit.

Praying in tongues

If a preacher asks you to pray in tongues, what meaning do you make of it? This statement prompts many 'Christians' to begin to speak an unknown language which they say is angelic or heavenly. As stated in the first work, I say again, as surely as the Lord lives before whom I stand, the God of the whole earth has nothing at all to do with this language wrapped as a gift of the Holy Spirit. He is of order, not of confusion.

Should any preacher ask you to pray in tongues, begin to pray in tongues; pray in languages which have meaning; pray in languages which you understand exactly what you are saying, and keep the usage of these in your private home. If you would pray in a tongue in a gathering of different tongue, keep your voice so low that the person beside you does not even hear you. Speak to yourself and to your God. Whenever my Lord would pray, even when He was alone, He would kneel before the Father and pray to Him quietly. The demons are not afraid of the loudness of your voice, it is the power behind the word you speak which makes them tremble; and that power is the Spirit of the Most High.

Paul wrote, "I will pray with my spirit and with understanding", meaning, he would rather pray in spirit, and in a tongue he fully understands. I know a bit of French, at least the greetings, but it would be disastrous to pray to God in this tongue, because I barely know a complete statement of request. I would rather use English then, or my native tongue when praying to God, so I can consciously communicate my needs to God.

Praying in tongues is praying in languages which you fully understand. If you would use a language which is alien to the rest in a gathering, use it silently. If you would lead them in prayers, use a language which is understood by everyone in the gathering, but if you must use a tongue different from theirs, then you either interpret into the language which they understand or find an interpreter. If there is no interpreter, keep it to yourself, and let another lead the prayer. I speak under the authority given to me by the One who has sent me that, all forms of communication in a language portrayed as angelic or heavenly is NOT of God. Do not be deceived.

In whose name shall we pray?

We pray to God who is a living God; the only living God. In whose name then do we pray? In the time of old, there was a way to reach God. The priests served as the link between the people, and God Almighty. At this time however, the elect can have a direct communication with God, just like it was before the fall. However, this time, we can only have access to God through the Way. It is written, I

(Christ Jesus) am the Way, the Truth, and the Life, no man can come to the Father except through Me. A name has been given unto us, which is above every other names, that at the mention of His name, every knee should bow, and every tongue must confess that Jesus Christ is Lord.

Since we can only have access and direct communication with God through the Way, then, we pray in His name; The Word of God. We pray in the name of Christ. One thing is to call on this name, another thing entirely is to be recognized by Him. Christ said, "Many will say to Me on that day, in your name we have done great things; we have prayed in your name and gotten answers, but I never knew them". Does the One you claim to call upon recognize you? Praying or doing wonders in His name is not sufficient proof that He knows or recognizes you. Notice, He said 'MANY', not few.

Being a time when knowledge has increased greatly, and deceit dominates the world, some have come to conclude that those who use the name 'Jesus' are bound for eternal damnation, because this was never the real name. Instead, He should be called by His name, 'Yeshua'. Do you not see what the devil is doing? No other name in the Scripture comes under such scrutiny except for the names he (the accuser) dreads; the names of God. Can you not see what the devil is doing? This is one of his works; the works of the flesh: to cause dissention and confusion among God's people. Indeed, many buy into his plan, but any true elect who has known the

Truth, and is being led by God's Spirit, will be unmoved by these tactics.

Why do you not call them Yirmeyah, Ysha'yah, or Mosheh? Why do you call these Jeremiah, Isaiah, and Moses? The latter is not their real names, do you not think? You hypocrites! You know to call the different language translations of the names of the prophets and apostles, but when it comes to the name which the devil fears, you create confusion among yourselves. You say it has to be in the Hebrew tongue. Who told you that the One who made all the languages in the world does not understand when you call upon Him in your language? These are the little tricks the devil plays on you when you do not have the knowledge of the True God. Since you pride in your knowledge and research, God has handed you over to him to be deceived.

Inasmuch you have no issue with calling Yirmeyah Jeremiah, which is the translation of the prophet's name in a language (English), you should not have issues with the name of my Lord, unless you are allowing the devil to use you.

The world used to be of a language, until the creation of the many languages by God Himself. Certainly, He expects you to pray in your tongue; in the language you understand. When the Word became flesh, He communicated with God in the language He understood. He had no problem with a language or the translation of a particular name. He knew the One He was praying to, and was never bothered by the right translation of names. Again I say, these are the little lies the devil uses to get you unsettled when you do not have the knowledge of the True God.

There are tons of names ascribed to the Holy One in my language, and these He recognizes. Jesus Christ went further to call Him 'Father', but God never rejected Him. It does not matter what you call; calling Yeshua or Yehoshua does not guarantee a place in heaven. The one who calls Yeshua and the one who calls Jesus Christ are in the same position; the only difference is that, they have called one person in different languages. And since God is the Creator of these languages, He will not despise one and give attention to the other on the basis that one called His name in Hebrew and the other has called in another language.

I am called Victor, yet if any man called me by this name in my local tongue 'Asegun' (literally translated, one who conquers), I would not despise him, its meaning is preserved and this is all that matters. If the other name He calls me by, Oluwatosin, translated as "God is worthy to be served", has a translation in Hebrew, or any other language, I would not despise it; so long its meaning, "God is worthy to be served", is preserved. So, if Jesus means, "God saves", then go ahead confidently and call on the name of your Lord in your language.

How effective is the name?

The Scripture says demons panic at the mention of the name. After fulfilling His mission, Jesus

Christ said, all power is given unto Him in heaven and on earth. Complete power and great authority. Now, there are two ways to ask a request from God; you could ask by naming the request and nothing more, or you could ask by naming the request and backing it with Jesus' name. The difference between the two is, one has the tendency of getting a quicker response than the other.

Two men go in unto a physician. The first man makes his complaints and pleads for immediate attention. The second man makes his complaint, backed up by the king's seal. Who gets answered first? The second man. It really is not about what the man says, but what accompanied his complaints. When you pray to God in Jesus' name, your requests have a higher chance of being answered. The name acts as a royal seal.

Power behind the name

The name itself carries power. It is the power behind it that causes demons to bow. The name and power behind it will be nothing in the mouth of a sinner. Before the name effectively makes demons bow, the power behind the name must be able to connect with the power within the one calling the name. If the name, Jesus, is backed by the Holy Spirit, then you need the same within you for the name to have any effect.

You could call on the name several times, yet there is no answer. Not that God is powerless, or cannot hear you, rather the reason for this is declared by God through the prophet Isaiah; behold, the Lord's hand is not short, that it cannot save; neither his ear heavy, that it cannot hear. But your iniquities have separated between you and your God, and your sins have hidden His face from you, that He will not hear. For your hands are defiled with blood, and your fingers with iniquity; your lips have spoken lies, your tongue has muttered perverseness. None calls for justice, nor any pleads for truth; rather, they trust in vanity, and speak lies; they conceive mischief, and bring forth iniquity. How then can you call on the name of the Holy One, and expect Him to hear you? Your transgressions are multiplied before God, and your sins testify against you; for your transgressions are with you, and as for your iniquities; you know them. In transgressing and lying against the Lord and His anointed, and departing away from God, speaking oppression and revolt, conceiving and uttering from the heart words of falsehood.

For demons to bow, you must have the same power within you. And you cannot have this power, unless your ways are right with God. Once, a group of people whose ways God knew not tried casting out a demon in Jesus' name. The demon responded, "I know the power behind these names you call upon, but the power within you I do not recognize". The name is powerful, but if you would successfully cast out a demon or do any miraculous act in that name, you must be backed by the same power backing the name.

The time of the end is a critical time. A period of deceit and gross wickedness. Here is what the Word says;

*"Then, if any man shall say
unto you, here is Christ, or there;
BELIEVE it NOT". Matthew
24:23*

*"For there shall arise false
Christs (note the plurality of it;
their numbers), and false
prophets, and shall show great
signs and wonders…" Matthew
24:24*

*"Wherefore if they shall say
unto you, behold, He is in the
desert (or on the mountain), do
not go: behold, He is in the
secret chambers; BELIEVE it
NOT". Matthew 24:26*

*"Many will say to me on
that (great and dreadful) day,
Lord, Lord, in your name I have
prophesied, cast out demons, and
done many wonderful works. And
I will respond to them, I never
knew you; depart from Me, you
workers of iniquity". Matthew
7:22-23*

Then,

*"But the Spirit expressly
states that in later times, some
will depart from faith, giving
heed to deceitful spirits, and
teachings of demons; speaking*

*lies in hypocrisy; having deaden
their own conscience". I Timothy
4:1-2*

*"Beloved, believe not every
spirit, but try the spirits whether
they are of God, because many
false prophets are gone out into
the world". I John 4:1*

These point out that false prophets do not stand before their audience calling on the devil; No. How would they successfully deceive MANY that way? They say they call on God. They tell you they have walked with, and have been called by God. But theirs is not the True God. Their kind of god is one who buys people over with gifts and tricks; one who multiplies signs and wonders in the same proportion as wickedness, immoralities, and iniquities abound. Their kind of god detests a clean temple, rather, it thrives in immoralities, and encourages the works of the flesh. Yet these ones appear to call on the name of the Lord.

Because those false prophets call on the name of the Lord, many automatically consider them an elect. Perhaps, you go over the highlighted texts above. This is exactly what has been prophesied to happen at this critical period of the world. Many appear to call on the name of the Lord, but this is not really what they call upon. But they keep you in the dark, and cover the mischief by the miracles they work moment later.

They successfully deceive many because there are many who are now led by sight. If an average individual saw a preacher perform wonders and miracles, the individual by default concludes that the preacher is being used greatly by God. You see the end products, but you do not see the power behind it. You do not know what he has done in his closet before coming out to work wonders.

But why would demons cast out demons? It is business, and they engage in it because of its high returns. If a man is afflicted by sickness, and the man finds Christ, then he gets saved, the devil considers that a major loss. For this reason, the devil also gives power to heal, but at the expense of that man's soul. The devil shows you he cares, but at the expense of your soul. He gives you gifts, and makes you comfortable, only because he has your soul.

That a preacher works wonders (at a time largely dominated by false prophets), is no proof that such is being used by God. That a preacher calls on the name of the Lord (at a time dominated by teachings of demons)is no proof that such is being inspired by the Holy Spirit. The devil gives gifts, and makes you comfortable. You will never be able to tell the difference as long as you are led by your flesh and by sight. If you would discern at this critical period and save your soul, then you must walk by faith; you must be led by the Spirit.

Indeed, spirits move during worship sessions in church gatherings, but have you stopped to ask what kind of spirit? Demonic ones particularly often appear violent and charismatic, but they have a way of operation that makes it seem like it is God's. God's Spirit, as you would see with the fruit of the Spirit, is gentle and peaceful. It is very much easier to believe in one being used by the devil than to believe one being used by the Most High. Inasmuch John, to whom God attested and revealed the identity of the Son of God, almost doubted at some point, how much more 'faint-hearted' 'believers', who are led by sight at a critical time such as this?

That a preacher calls on God's name is not enough. Check the fruit he bears. Certainly, as long as any man has not the indwelling of God's Spirit, such man is vulnerable to falling for the deceits going on in the end-time. The elect are the ones who are kept safe from being washed off; for they know the truth, and are grounded in the knowledge of the True God.

Chapter 2

The Lord's Prayer: Thanksgiving

When we pray, we should start it off by giving thanks to God. It was not by chance that this template starts off with God, specifically, giving thanks and reverence. This follows the pattern, "(even in your prayers), seek first the kingdom of God…" Clearly, He did not give this out, then acted otherwise; He followed this pattern Himself.

Our Father in heaven:

Normally, when we write a (formal) letter, what comes before the body of the letter is the name or title of the one to whom it is addressed. In fact, this is the most important part of the whole message. Imagine starting off with your requests, and after an epistle, the name or address of the receiver is left out. This kind of letter either ends in the bin or in the wrong hands.

Therefore, before ANYTHING at all, it should be stated in clear language to whom your prayer is addressed. Jesus Christ not only gave the name of the receiver, but the address as well. Name: (Our Father); Address: Heaven. You will not find a better address than that. Many people make different requests every day. As you commune with fellow humans, some commune with spirit, and powers. When you start off your prayers without naming the receiver, even demons can eavesdrop whatever you say. The moment you name the one your communication is to, others are blocked out. They see you pray, but they know not what you ask.

Hallowed by your name;

Having named your receiver, proceed to worship. He is not like other gods. He has eyes, and can see. He has ears and can hear. He has hands and can save. Above all, while other gods thrive in darkness and iniquity, He is the Father of light. All of these set Him totally apart from other gods. As you start off your prayer session, appreciate these attributes of Him. In your praises and thanksgiving, let it be known that you are praying to the One who is unrivalled.

Most importantly, make sure your worship meets God's standard of an acceptable worship, as detailed in the work "Praise". Ensure the temple is undefiled, the altar pure, and the worshipper (you) consecrated and purified.

Your kingdom come;

While writing a letter could be largely one-sided, prayer is not strictly designed that way. It should be a communication. Remember when you started the prayer, you did not address yourself as a slave or one without any worth to the receiver. You did say, Father; like a son would call on his father. This Father, as stated earlier, though invisible, is

One who has mouth and can talk, He has ears and can hear. This is a way of inviting Him over to the 'discussion room'. In other words, you are inviting Him over to take charge of what you shall say, and how it is said. Simply put, this is a way of welcoming His presence.

Also, this part portrays how vigilant one is in preparation for His coming kingdom. Once, Some say, "Oh, Christ should not return yet. I still have to complete my education, get married, and start a family". If you are in this category, would you not say you have lost sight on the second coming of Christ? Can you still confidently say you are looking forward to His coming, and would be ready at any time He comes?

The apostles knew the gospel had not yet reached all the nations (during their time), yet, they wrote and charged the brethren as though they were already in the end time. They wrote as though, all the signs came to pass already, and Christ would return any moment from then. Yet, they knew the end (which Christ Himself spoke of) had not yet come. They were conscious because they kept the saying sin their hearts. They were constantly looking forward to that great day of the Lord. They had been crucified with Christ, and had forsaken the ways of the flesh.

So, when you say your prayers, and even in the earliest part, you say "your kingdom come, Lord", this shows how conscious you are. It also serves as a reminder that this place is temporal. Your home is up, and you patiently and consciously await the day when you are called home. You see how an individual who is led by the flesh cannot please God? He who lives in the flesh thinks more of earth than things above. He who is led by the Spirit is consistently looking forward to going home.

Your will be done on earth as it is done in heaven;

This is just as important as the others mentioned so far; maybe, as equally important as the address of the recipient. This part is often taken out when individuals pray to God, and taking this part out is like digging a pit for yourself. This is largely because our mortal self does not know how to pray or what to pray for. It is the Spirit which helps. Our flesh can hardly make a difference between needs and wants. Oftentimes, we want things which could destroy us; particularly for those who are led by the flesh. Hence, it is very important that this part of the template is not left out.

The statement "your will be done on earth as it is done in heaven" can be taken in two ways; first, it could be taken on a personal note, "Lord, above all my requests, let your will alone prevail." In other words, do not grant those requests which are beneficial to my flesh at the expense of my spiritual growth. Secondly, the statement could be taken generally, "Lord, as it is done in heaven, let your will also be done on earth". We shall look at the personal first.

The role of this particular statement, "let your will alone be done" cannot be overlooked. This part of the prayer gives you the 'license' to ask for anything and everything because, in the end, only those things which you need would be granted. While I was growing up, there is a specific prayer that the Lord God would always lead me to say, "Father, let Your will alone be done in my life". Hardly do I hold a session without that popping up on the list. By the time I was in my late teenage years, I never bothered about anything anymore. I did not have to go to God every time I reached a crossroad, or needed to make a decision. I just took the decision; oftentimes, I did not even understand why I had gone for a particular choice, but when I saw the outcome months or years later, I figured out I could never have made such sound decisions on my own.

Sometime ago, I said to someone, "when people (who know me closely) see me, they think I am wise and full of vision..." this person cut in affirming that was undoubtedly true, then I proceeded, "...but, I am not. In fact, I am foolish". I further explained this; people see me do things and think it is I who do them, when in fact it is not. Let Him leave me, then you realize I am really nothing and empty. All I do is follow instructions. Things I do are never a function of my mental reasoning or strategic planning, but what He leads and instructs me to do. But since He works behind the scenes, men ascribe the praise to me, when I do not deserve a bit of it.

What I am now, and what I have been able to do are direct function of the request, "Let your will alone be done in my life", because the life I live is no longer mine. Like a leaf being tossed by the wind.

Even till this point, He still instructs me to say this prayer, but less frequent than many years ago.

Jesus Christ made only two requests in one of His prayer sessions. One of these requests is, "Not as I will, but let your will be done". This is how important this part is. If you have to make two or three requests, let one of them be, "above all, let your will be done, Lord". If you have to ask only ONE request, then the request should be, "Let your will alone be done, Lord".

When you bring your own will under subjection to God's will, you make the burden easier. God's will is not always comfortable for the flesh which lives in the present and is a lover of comfort and worldly pleasures. The major reason why you would hardly find the prophets or the apostles going before God every time a storm arose and they needed to make a big decision is because, they were completely operating under the will of the Most High. They had the mind of God; the life they lived was no longer theirs, and even in trials, temptation, and persecution, they were unshaken; for they knew, nothing unpleasant would have befallen them if God had not allowed it. So, whatever came their way, they did not complain nor think of it as God failing them. Paul was thrown in prison, likewise Peter, and Joseph. Have you seen how peaceful and settled they were; insomuch that Peter rather slept, and Joseph was made chief among the inmates? In his state, he gave hope to the hopeless, strength to the weak, and he was a problem solver to the rest of the inmates.

The major challenge is, how to distinguish between God's will and self will. The latter is the will of self, often driven by your flesh and senses, while God's will is God's own plan for you as written and established from the foundations of the world. This vessel, from the time the earth was formed, has been destined to walk this earth at this time to carry out the purpose of God. This was and is God's intention, and at no point, for whatsoever reason, would He change it. One has said, oftentimes God changes what He has planned and written for us to what we want, so far it brings Him glory. Do not be deceived by false teachers. It is you, having arrived here, who begin to get distracted by the activities and progress of others, the values of the world, and the sight which you see generally. Then, you pick for yourselves careers not minding whether it is His will. Nevertheless, you deceive yourself, saying, this makes me fulfilled and I bring God glory. Even the one who helps in painting a temple to suit worldly standards says what he does glorifies God. He says he beautifies God's temple. Shall we make it pagan for the sake of beautifying?

What is the will of God, and how does it differ from self-will? It is either of the two; you are what you are now from the different choices you have made from the past, even so, your future rests solely on the choices you make from this point or the ones you have made. These choices are largely influenced by either of two forces—your flesh, or God's Spirit. There is a constant internal war between your flesh and your spirit. The more one influences your choices, the weaker the other gets. You do not see, but this is a daily struggle between the two. For instance, you want to stay away from a bad habit. You make the decision to stay away, then, few hours later, there is a conflict within you to try it out again. You eventually repeat the act saying, this is the last time, I will never try it again after this. But, sometime later, you still get back to doing it. The spirit is always willing, but the flesh is weak. If you are ruled by flesh and fleshly desires, your spirit becomes too weak to prevent abominations penetrating the temple wall. If you are governed by the Spirit, you will not fulfil the lust of the flesh.

God's will or Self will?

Many pray recklessly without minding if their request eventually becomes their bane. They think of what is good, develop the desire to have it, and they pray for it as though their life is dependent on it. They pray for long life (after all, it is written, God will satisfy you with long life). They pray for financial prosperity (since it is written, beloved I wish above all things that you may prosper…). Every of their requests is backed up with a verse from the Scriptures; it matters less if these quotations are wrongly applied or misinterpreted.

How do you know that what you pray for is the will of God? Every day, you seem to have a long list of prayers waiting, but then, how do you know that it is His will and not the desire of your own flesh? Many are quick to say, it is written in the Scriptures; open to this and that. But then, are your Scripture quotations not a blessing for keeping God's commandments? Once when I visited certain gatherings, the shepherds would often pronounce upon his sheep the blessings in Deuteronomy 28, and the gathering would claim them. But they are not told that these blessings will not come except they obey and keep God's commandments. When it is said, "keep the Sabbath", you are quick to say, "the law is done away with; we live in the period of grace, thus no longer under the burden of the law". You have spoken well. But why do you not say the same when a blessing attached to this law is pronounced upon you? Should you not also say, "we will not say 'amen' because these blessings are for keeping the law and they are no longer applicable in our time"? You stay away from the requirement, but want to get the benefits. You want to reap where you have not sown. If you claim the prayers, then definitely, the curse also be upon you if you fail to keep the law and statutes.

---

*"Now it shall come to pass,
if you **diligently obey** the **voice** of
the **Lord** your God, **to observe**
carefully **ALL His**
commandments which I
command you today, that the
Lord your God will set you high
above all nations of the earth.
And **all these blessings** shall
come upon you and overtake you,
because you **obey** the voice of
the Lord your*

God."Deuteronomy 28:1-2
NKJV

You follow the leading of your flesh, desiring what is good and pleasing, but unwilling to keep the commandments of the Lord. Christ did ask for the cup to pass, but that was not the will of the Father. Elijah did say, take my life; for I am not better than the ones before me, but this was not the will of God. As we are in the flesh, it is not unusual that we would often make requests contrary to God's will for our lives.

The way of the flesh and its will is that of pleasure and no hurt. This is why you pray evils away more than you ask for grace to overcome temptations and trials when they come. When people pray, they say the Spirit of God said to say this particular prayer, when in fact, it is their flesh leading them on. You want to live comfortably and in wealth and so, you say prayers related to that, unknown to you that these are primarily your fleshly desires.

You pursue a career because you picked interest, but you say it is God's will. You get married to someone and say, it is God's will. Now, when you encounter problems with these choices you blame God, but you ought to blame yourself. You take responsibility because you have followed your own will.

Oftentimes, when you pray, you highlight your wants. You cannot correctly tell between wants and needs, so, you just pray as you like. Every time you include in your prayers that God's will prevails, you have done it right. You need not worry about praying amiss. Because you have said this, when the fire burns it gets rid of requests whose fulfilment would have brought you harm, therefore, what's left to go up to God are the requests of yours which are in line with His will for you.

Chapter 3

The Lord's Prayer: Request

Once you are done with giving thanks to God, you proceed to making your requests. Since you have sincerely placed God's will above yours, then you should not bother whether a request is right or not. If it is, it will be granted. If your request contradicts God's will, it will not be granted. And when it is not granted, you know not to doubt God's power but to trust in His will and plans for you. When He does not do what you ask (because your request contradicts His plans), but you go on to question His abilities or get really disappointed, then your wish to have His will above yours was insincere.

Give us today our daily bread.

It is said that the basic needs are food, clothing, and shelter. In a way, this has to do with asking for the provision of your NEEDS. What does the Scripture say? The Lord will fill up your NEEDS according to His riches in glory through Christ Jesus. Note that it mentions the necessities only. Many often quote this part of the Scripture to justify any request that they make, saying, God is willing to supply ALL. But, is that what He really said?

Needs are necessities; those things you cannot possibly live without. If you go days without food, you cannot function properly, and if it draws even longer, one could die. If one is homeless, it would be difficult to survive. How would the person cope when it rains heavily or when a strong wind blows? Being homeless also makes one vulnerable to attacks. Clothing is just as equally important. No man who is sane could walk around naked. These are the things that, if you do not have them, survival would be difficult and many of your achievements would be impossible.

Wants are desires; those things you wish to have even though the lack of them would not kill you. I could want a car for different reasons. If I do not own a car, it will not hurt me a bit, neither will it hinder the works which I do, still, my flesh would trick me into thinking that, the car is something which I need. Of course, owning a car makes movement easier and faster, but still, it is my own desire, not a necessity.

When Christ talked about provisions and supplies, He was clearly talking about needs, and God does not deny us of this. Everything outside feeding, clothing, and shelter, is wants and desires. And desires differ from one individual to another. When you make requests in your prayers, let it be limited to your NEEDS. If, eventually, there is a want that you actually need in order to fulfil His purpose, He will make it available to you even without you asking.

Many get themselves in troubles because of the requests that they make. A job looks attractive to you, and you begin to covet the position. You promise to get it at any cost, and so, you pray and continue to pray. At this point, you have already made it clear from your actions that you do not care what God's will is, getting the job is of more importance to you. You eventually get the job, and if you get into any trouble later on, you return to ask God questions. You remind Him how you have faithfully paid your tithes and offerings, but then, was it not you who chose not to submit to the will of the One who knows tomorrow?

You see a man, and because you are led by your flesh, you just want to settle down with him. You are asked to pray about it, and you actually do. You pray about it even though you have made up your mind to marry him. What do you expect your heart to say? Since you have made up your mind already before making inquiry from Him, you have clearly stated that His opinion does not count, therefore, He grants your request. Later on, a stumbling block is before you, and the relationship seems to be heading down the drain, then you go back to God in prayers asking why He is watching things get messier, or why He had let you get into the union in the first place. Did you not make the choice yourself? At the start, you did not tell Him because you honestly cared about His will, rather, you told Him so He could affirm your choice. Now you have made this mess yourself, but expecting God to take responsibility. Why do you not take responsibility for your own actions and choices?

When you make your requests, it is safe to stick to your needs only. Do not assume you need because you may not realize when your flesh is leading you to make a request. As for your wants, ask God for His will to be done.

It is good to pray, even the Scripture says to pray without ceasing. Yet, I tell you assuredly, if you live righteously in accordance with the commandments of God, you will not have to ask for a thing before it is done. I'm not talking about money (wealth) and cars, as these are often wants. But, as far as your needs are concerned, if your way pleases God, your needs would be made readily available without you asking. This is so because God does not deny His own anything that they need. This is highlighted below, in Christ's words.

---

*"Therefore I say to you, **Do not worry** about your life, what you will eat or what you will drink; nor about your body, what you will put on. Is not life more than food and the body more than clothing? Look at the birds of the air, for they neither sow nor reap nor gather into barns; yet your heavenly Father feeds them. Are you not of more value than they? Which of you by worrying can add one hour to his lifespan? So why do you worry about clothing? Consider the lilies of the field, how they grow: they neither toil nor spin; and yet*

I say to you that even Solomon in all his glory was not arrayed like one of these. Now if God so clothes the grass of the field, which today is, and tomorrow is thrown into the furnace, will He not much more clothe you, O you of little faith? Therefore do not worry, saying, 'What shall we eat?' or 'What shall we drink?' or 'What shall we wear?' For after all these things the Gentiles seek. **For your heavenly Father knows that you NEED all these things.** *But seek first the kingdom of God and His righteousness, and all these things shall be added to you."*
Matthew 6:25-33

Do ask for your needs in your requests, but surely, if you truthfully seek His kingdom first and obey all that He has commanded you, you will not have to ask Him before He meets the needs.

Forgive our transgressions as we forgive those who sin against us.

Notice that this one comes with a condition. As we forgive the ones who sin against us, forgive us our shortcomings as well. Remember the parable, where a certain servant was forgiven by his master. Now, when he went out he saw another servant who was indebted to him. Even though the servant owed him less than what he owed the master yet the master had pardoned him, he was not merciful as he had been shown mercy. He condemned his debtor, and because he did this, the master remembered his own sins also and convicted him.

Some pray but in their heart they hold a grudge against another. When some have misunderstandings with another, they would say, "nothing would ever make me forgive him."If you say you will not have mercy, will God not remember your own sins as well? Is it not written that the ones who show mercy shall likewise obtain mercy from God? What does the Word say? Christ said, if you will burn incense to God, and at that point you remember how your brother offended you and you have not forgiven him, go quickly and forgive him, then return to make your offerings to God. Make peace before your offering could be acceptable in God's sight.

You see, forgiveness of sin is very much important that it is a part of the requests stated in the prayer guide. The act of asking for forgiveness is like purifying yourself before you make your offering. Praying without asking for forgiveness is like a priest going into the temple to burn incense on the altar without first purifying himself. If the priest then be impure, the impurity pollutes the entire offering, and so, God does not give regard to such.

Make an inquiry into your past, has there been someone who did you such evil that you have since determined never to forgive? If there is, now is the time to let go. Remember, God has always forgiven your sins, despite how great the debts have been. Your refusal to let go only gives the accuser an edge over your soul. Why do you even punish your own self by keeping the grudge in your heart? Would you let them hurt you twice? They have hurt you once or more, but then would you allow them to rob you of eternal rest? No matter how great the sin is, it sure is not worth an eternity of torment. If you will save your soul and have eternal rest, you must bring your flesh under subjection, and choose to make peace with the ones who have sinned against you.

It would be wrong to pray to God without asking for the forgiveness of sins. Also, it would be self-destructive if you asked God to forgive your sins when you knowingly have not forgiven another who has sinned against you. While the former stops your offering (prayers) from getting to God as God has said through Isaiah, the latter could bring about your own destruction since he could go to God to accuse you of seeking forgiveness when you have refused to forgive your neighbour. Forgive the ones who sin against you, then ask God to forgive your own sins, you can then proceed to burn incense to God.

Lead us not into temptation.

Many take this to mean, temptations and trials are not for God's people. But the intent of this request is not to pray never to be tempted, but to pray that you never fall for temptation. These are two different things. You should not pray that temptations do not come, if you do, when they come you will not be able to deal with them. You only overcome when you are prepared to take it on. For one whose coming is unanticipated, it is easier to fall than to stand. So, here, before you ask Him for lots of money and car, a very crucial point of your requests should be, "help me Lord never to fall for temptation."

Hardly would you find someone who still includes this in their requests. Yet, for anyone who is watchful and vigilant, this is an indispensable part of their requests. Many are caught in the moment seeking comfort and praying for breakthrough, but this part about overcoming temptations never makes the list. What meaning do you make of His words when He said to keep watch? You do not know when the enemy comes, and so you must be vigilant and be at watch always. But instead of watch, what you do is to dig for yourself a pit which makes it rather easier to fall into temptation.

How do you keep watch? Why do you keep watch? If you know why you keep watch, maybe you would do it more effectively; for your enemy, the devil, walks about without rest like a fierce lion looking for whom to devour. If your enemy does not rest but is rather after your soul, why should you let your guard down? You keep watch because the accuser is watching you, looking for that time you are most vulnerable so he could spoil. Many are they who have fallen at the time of the end. They fell asleep at watch, and the devil attacked. Despite coming together as a unit, they were outnumbered and great was their fall. Now their eyes are opened, having been fed with false knowledge, they are cast out of the presence of the Lord.

How do you keep watch? You keep watch by praying and through putting up measures in preparation against attack. Deception is when you are told that temptations would not come. If you are a follower of Christ walking through the compressed way, how could you not partake of the tribulation and temptations? Was He not tempted? Has He also died to take away temptations and trials? If the owner of the house is aware that the robber comes at a certain hour, he goes in and prays every night, then off to bed, without any measures put up, will the thief not eventually catch him at the hour he is asleep? If the owner of the house be aware of an impending attack, and he prays, and puts up measures; limiting his period of rest and continuously checking to know when the danger approaches, will he not have an edge?

There are many who cannot even identify a temptation. Christ was hungry, and you'd almost consider it natural and usual for someone with so much power to want to transform a stone into bread. But He was vigilant, and He knew how God works, and so, could clearly distinguish when it was the Spirit, and when it was not. Many learn to pray these days; they go hours praying not to fall, but they fall nonetheless. They know how to pray, but not how to follow it up with actions as directed. If you had a property, and there are trespassers, do you continually pray in your closet that they do not walk on your property or you go out, make an edge round about, preventing the movement of those trespassers?

You do not want to fall. You continuously pray for God to uphold you, yet, when the opposite sex invites you over to their place, though you know you two would be alone, you honour the invitation nonetheless. You think you are strong enough to withstand the temptation? You have seen the pit, and have chosen to fall into it.

When you say this prayer, the Spirit of God guides you and feeds your thoughts with measures. He helps you to build high walls (standards; dos/don'ts) so that when the attack comes, your temple is impenetrable. When it comes to dealing with temptations, it is not enough to pray in your closet, you must follow it up with certain acts as the Spirit leads you. You have read, FLEE all forms of sexual immorality. Imagine Joseph staying there and praying continuously that her master's wife's heart be changed, or, rebuking her on the spot when she tried to get him to lie with him. Have you not read how the mighty have fallen, and the wisdom of the wise brought to nought by this wine?

You deliberately take for yourselves sex partners, yet you claim to be awake and on guard, oh, how deceived you are. Every day, in this present world, an average individual is faced with at least one temptation; temptation to tell lies, or to cheat, or to steal, or to bear false witness, or to commit sexual immorality, or to sin with your heart, or to conform to worldly standards, or to make for oneself idols, or to permit an abominable act in one's temple. Every hour comes with its own temptation, and the one who is not keeping watch is in danger. Pray at all times that God keeps you out; not that He would not permit the tempter to come at all, but that He would always make you victorious when you are tempted. Most importantly, when you pray, set up measures so that you may withstand the attacks of the evil one.

Deliver us from evil.

Besides provision of one's basic needs, and asking for help to stay on guard so one does not depart from the faith, this covers the last basic request; protection. The world is filled with evil, and it is evident now, and in the coming years of trials when evil rules the heart of men. Deliver us from evil is one elaborated by David, saying, I will say of the Lord, that He is my refuge and my fortress. Surely, He will deliver me from the snare of the fowler and from the perilous plagues. With His feathers He shall cover me, and under His wings I will take refuge. I shall not be afraid of the terror by night nor of the arrow that flies by day, nor of the plagues that walk in darkness, nor of the destruction that makes desolate at midday. No evil shall befall me, neither shall any plague come near my dwelling.

Noteworthy that David clearly understood what many do not at the time of the end. Many like to read the Psalms, and the Scriptures generally, saying "amen" to the blessings and rejecting the curses, but are the blessings not a reward for obedience? Particularly, when you talk about God's protection, there is something you have to do first. When you do, then you are certainly going to enjoy His protection. TRUST GOD! If you put your trust in God completely, then this is what you get in return.

This vessel cannot recall the last time he has prayed to God asking for protection. It is good to ask, but assuredly I say, if you trust God with the whole of your heart, you will not need to ask before He protects you. Though I do not, yet I tread on paths other men dare not tread; for they think, it is not safe. But I tread not for showoffs, but of the absolute trust I have in the One who leads me. He guides me to where I must be at the time I need to be there. I take no thought for my safety because He is my safety.

Many claim to trust God with their mouth, but they really do not. They trust their money instead. They trust God 'wholly' only when their money or whatever they pride in has failed them. If you are afflicted by some disease, what is the first thing you do? You seek medical intervention. Even if you pray that God heals you, it does not stop you from seeking the help of men. You say, the spiritual has its place so does the medical, let not one interfere with the other. When some have spent, but it does not get better, then they know to 'trust' God. But is that really trust, or taking God as your last resort? You only trust God when He is the only option you have got.

If your trust in God is not whole, how would you stand in the coming years? When evil strikes, and the arrows fly by, would you not side with the devil just to save your own flesh? The hour comes when the patience and endurance of the elect is tested. Whether you are for God or not, it will be made known. Pray that you be delivered from evil, but you must do your part by trusting God. Some say God has sent them yet go out in the company of armed men. Is your god not mighty to save you? If you claim to serve the true God, then you do not trust Him with your safety; for your peace is in the hands of your men. As long as you have them, you feel at rest. If you do not have them, and you walk in the midst of the people, would you confidently walk with peace in your mind? If your trust is in flesh, how then can you claim to trust God?

Trust the Lord your God with all your heart, and watch how He fights on your behalf. Did He not for Moses, or Christ, or the apostles? When you pray, follow up your prayers with actions. You could fast and pray fervently never to fall into temptation, yet, the next hour, you fall into one. You could pray fervently for protection, yet you meet with evil. Why? Because though you pray, your trust is actually not in the Lord. You deceive yourselves by honouring God with your lips, when your heart is far away from the true God

Basically, when you pray, the key indispensable parts of your requests should be provision of basic needs, help to stay on guard and to overcome temptations, forgiveness of your sins (which could actually affect the whole of your worship and make it unacceptable if skipped), and lastly, protection from evil. Anything outside these are wants, for this cause should you include in your prayers your total submission to the will of God. Thus, even if your flesh leads you to say a certain prayer, when the fire burns, it filters out requests which contradict God's plans.

Chapter 4

Bringing your prayer to an end.

Notice how this template starts and how it ends—Thanksgiving; it ends in giving thanks. You start by giving thanks and you end by giving thanks. Now, this is how the prayers of the elect should go. When you pray, you start by giving thanks to God even before making your requests known. This is the basis for your creation. Your prayers should not be requests only. As a priest, when you pray, you burn incense to God from your heart. Prayers going alongside thanksgiving is like combining two or more different spices. Specifically, your thanksgiving is that spice with the strongest scent when lit up. The more of this spice, the more pleasing your offering is. Now, if you took out the thanksgiving or your requests are evidently much more than your thanksgiving, how would your offering look, how pleasant will its scent be? How lasting would it be going up before God? When they came out from Egypt, they gave thanks. David likewise made it a habit to give thanks. What was Paul and Silas doing in prison? They were giving thanks. See how vital thanksgiving is. At the start, give thanks. At the end of your requests, give thanks. In all things, give thanks; for this is the will of the Father.

For Yours is the kingdom, and the power and the glory for the ages, amen.

God has created us for His glory. He has created us so we would bring Him glory, and one of the ways you do this is through thanksgiving. Your worship is very important to God. It should clearly reflect the glory of the Lord, not the glory or the gratification of your flesh. When you pray, do not pray like the fleshly who like to pray in the eye sight of men, that they may be perceived as prayerful. Surely, these ones have their reward. But when you pray, either you choose to say your prayers in your heart or verbally, do it in sincerity and in your closet. The God who sees you in secret will reward you openly. When you give thanks, in songs or statements, do not be like the fleshly who put their carnal pleasures before their service to God; for these ones love to sing to God the way the world sing to their idols because this way is pleasing to their senses. But you, when you give thanks, give thanks sincerely and from a consecrated heart.

God's is the kingdom, and all power ultimately belongs to Him. Nothing happens without His knowledge, and He sits on His throne doing as He pleases. His is the ultimate power, and He directs the affairs of the whole earth. He has the power to save and to destroy, the power to take one up, and put the other down. If He wishes, He could shut the heavens so that there is no rain in the land, and if it pleases Him, He could send rain in abundance. The rain comes in its season, and the works of nature evidently show His might.

Again I say to you, let the glory of the Lord be your focus, not the gratification of your flesh. Many pick an act from the world, fine-tuning it to fit a misinterpreted part of the Scripture. They say, "it matters not what we do, as long as it is done to the glory of the Lord, it is fine; God is fine with it, and who are you to judge?"Did God truly say He was fine with it? If that is, then that cannot be my own God. He takes no pleasure in the works of the flesh, neither is He glorified in it. What you claim to do to the glory of God, is it really done to God's glory or for the gratification of your flesh? How can you be sure that the voice which gave you the go-ahead to act in the ways of the world is not the voice of the deceiver? Do you not know that when you make an inquiry from God, the answer you get is the same you perceived to be right when your flesh is in control?

If you claim to do what you do to the glory of God, then, you will carefully seek what worship God takes pleasure in. Let your thanksgiving be done in due reverence to God, and in sincerity.

Chapter 5

Prayers and Misconceptions

Prayers are generally thought to be a way of communicating with God. This narrow view forces many to focus primarily on themselves when they pray. Thanksgivings are optional, and they ask for several things that they want, often quoting, "till now, you have asked nothing. Ask, and keep asking until your joy is full." When you consider your prayers as incense, however, this shifts the focus from self to God. Your prayer is the offering you make, the incense you burn to God. You would need the Holy Spirit, as your form of worship cannot be transformed without Him. Think of Aaron, when he goes into the holy place to burn incense on the altar, on whom was his focus; God or himself?

When you pray, having the Spirit of God rule your heart, your prayers go up to God as incense. When you understand this as an act of worship, then you know your offering would be incomplete without thanksgiving. Because many people think of prayer as a way to communicate only and to pour out the entirety of their problems before God, they often focus mainly on themselves and so the only thing they do through the prayer session is make requests. But where is that precious spice with stronger pleasant smell when burned? This is taken out or a little added. Your prayer is an act of worship to God, and so, your focus should be on God. Even if you make no request, God would not sit back and do nothing. He will take care of your basic needs.

Prayers: Spiritual warfare

For the weapons of our warfare are not carnal, but mighty through Christ, Paul writes. For this reason, many live recklessly, and when judgement eventually comes, they resort to praying. Some would even stay without food, praying fervently. If you lived a Godly life, would you fall under attacks? Is it not written, if the ways of a man please God, He will make even his enemies be at peace with him? Let me show you why you consistently fall under attacks.

Your body is the temple, and your soul is the priest within it. Think of yourself in a house. Outside of the house are thieves and destroyers who lie in wait. They cannot come inside because you have locked the entrances from behind. They continue to look for ways, but since the entrances are the only entry point, and it is not something they can open, they stay around waiting for the day you will open. You know there are forces outside, but you have been locked inside for too long. You think that it is boring (Does having to serve God have to be boring? Why should the non-believers have fun while the believers endure a 'dull' atmosphere in the name of not conforming to worldly standards? You ask), and you want to check outside for a minute. You have been kept safe all along, and no need to worry about a thing. However, the moment you open that door (wanting to relax the confinement a bit), a thief sneaks in. Your life has been peaceful all through, but the moment they enter, chaos starts.

Since the thief does not come but for to steal, to kill, and to destroy, the thief starts off by stealing your health, and subsequently, your joy. You resort to prayers. When something unsettles you or takes your joy, you pray like you never would again. Would the thief have entered if you had not opened the door for it? You have brought the disaster upon yourself, yet you pray, expecting God to eliminate the thief immediately. You would even ask God, why, why He had allowed that? Did God open that door or you did?

You venture into sin, disregarding God's commandments because of the lust of the eyes, and when a demon sneaks in, you question God why He has allowed it. But it was not God, it was you who invited the demon in. Many of the battles you fight through prayers would have been prevented only if you had diligently kept God's commandments. If you live according to God's will and statutes, you will not have to face these consistent battles. Once the thief is done with stealing the treasures, he starts to aim for your life, to kill. Eventually, his target is to destroy one's soul. Many fall into the pits they dig and blame it on the devil. "The devil is a liar", you say. But you are the liar, and the devil your father.

It has been long since this vessel made such requests. If this vessel got sick today, I would not question God on his behalf nor ask for healing. Rather, he reviews his past actions, trying to figure out how he has fallen short. Because, if he got sick, it must be a punishment for his sins; letting in an abomination into my host.

You have a problem, and the first thing you most certainly do is pray. Sometimes, though you pray, nothing gets better. Then you are deceived, thinking that God does not answer prayers. I will show you what is.

When that thief enters, and causes you discomfort, what is the FIRST thing you do? Declare war against it? If this is your first response, you will get overwhelmed in time. The first response when you notice such invasion should be to SHUT THE ENTRANCE (which you have opened). Close that door first to prevent many more from coming in. When the door is shut, you know you have got only one foe to face. However, when you leave the door open, facing the one, by the time you are done conquering, three more have entered. As you face the three, many more enter.

When you sin, and you invite problems into your life, you begin to pray. Instead of correcting your ways, and making your path straight before God, you choose to pray. By the time this issue is resolved, you see another has risen that requires your attention. When was the last time you prayed to God without a problem bothering you? When was the last time you went to God in prayer thanking Him only because there was nothing to ask for?

You continue to have problems, not necessarily because many are the afflictions of the righteous,

rather because you continue to let in these demons
by your own hands.

You commit fornication, and a demon torments
you as a result. Instead of shutting the door and
discontinuing the act of fornication, you rather tackle
that demon in prayers. I tell you assuredly, even if
you win, you will have many more foes because you
have continued to commit sexual immoralities.
Because of your sins you are always faced with
battles. You resolve one, and another begins. Don't
be too quick to pray, reflect on your actions. Does
your way please God?

Poverty, Wealth, and Prayers.

It's a common belief that the poor spends more
time praying than the rich. If two men were in the
same gathering, one with wealth and the other poor.
Then, the preacher asks them to say a particular
prayer (say, a prayer for breakthrough, or to fend off
demonic attacks), you find the rich man standing
upright, and praying in such a calm manner—you
barely hear what he says, and if the prayer session
draws on for too long, he likely loses interest or sits
down for sometime—while the poor man moves up
and down, shaking his head, and praying at the top
of his voice. If you watch a group of Europeans pray,
and you compare them to the way a gathering of
Africans pray, this becomes clear. For this reason,
many think, when you are poor it means you are not
Godly. This is why you have too many problems to
take up to God at once. But that is a misconception.

Having money or not has nothing to do with
your relationship with God. The rich is not any

[52]

closer to God than the poor is. The only reason a poor man prays more is because his faith is in prayers. The rich pray less not because they have no problems at all, instead, they pray less because they trust in their money. As they say, "money answers all things."

If a poor man's son is found guilty of theft, the poor man is thrown into disarray, and since he knows no man, he turns to God. If he is asked to pray and fast for twenty and one days for mercy, he is willing to. The man prays for that long and at the end, his son gets a light punishment (say, community service). Compare to the son of a rich man who is found guilty of murder. Once the rich man hears, he makes calls to the rest of his kind in top position. He visits the concerned parties with cash, and in the end, the son mysteriously gets away with it. Both the rich and the poor have found themselves in similar situation, in fact, the rich man's was messier, yet, while it took one twenty and one days praying, the other resolved it within hours.

If a poor man notices an unusual bump around his neck, and after praying but nothing happens, he makes an appointment with the doctor. The doctor tells him after the diagnosis, "I'm sorry to break this, but it is the early signs of a deadly disease, and it is best you get it removed while it is still early. It will cost around six million naira." The poor man returns home, phones his pastor, and what does he do? He prays. There is nothing God cannot do, and so, he prays for hours asking for healing. If a rich man notices something unusual and after visiting his

doctor he is told, "Sir, this is one of the early signs
of a deadly disease. It will cost six million naira to
get it removed." On that spot, the rich man is already
setting a date to get the problem out.

When the poor falls sick, he prays first. When
he prays and it looks like it's worse than before, then
he makes the move to get himself treated through
other means. When a rich man falls sick, without
any delay, he makes his way to the hospital to get
treated.

Jesus Christ said, it is easier for a camel to go
through the eye of a needle than it is for a rich man
to enter into God's kingdom. Not because it is not
possible, but for the nature of man. The rich
absolutely put their trust in their money. The only
time they trust God is when the money has failed
them. You may be rich, and claim to trust God, but
your claim falls apart when you are brought close to
the standard. When you fall sick, the first thought
that comes to mind is to sick medical intervention.
When a rich man does this, yet it gets worse, then
such is brought before God.

To many, trust in God is like a fallback plan.
Your main focus and trust is in the money you have.
You think your money will solve all your problems.
Your money is your god. The only reason why the
poor seem to absolutely trust God is because that is
the only option available to them. If the poor man in
the instances above becomes wealthy, he will tread
in the same path as the rich man. Those problems
which used to cost him hours of prayers would be
easily taken care of by money.

The length of your prayers does not necessarily imply that you are far away from God. Since the rich pray less, would it mean they are closer to God than the poor? Not so. The rich pray less because they resolve most of their problems with money, and the little that cannot be resolved in this manner are brought before God.

Your closeness and uprightness with God should not be measured by your wealth, but by the problems and challenges you face. How often are you afflicted? How often do you fall sick? Are your moments of sorrow more than your joyful moments? Do you often have to deal with one problem or the other? If you face problems and challenges from time to time, regardless of your economic status, you need to watch it! It means you are living in sin, and demons continue to make their way in through that leak.

Prayers for prosperity

It is a perilous time, and rather than diligently watch out for the Lord's return, many are busy striving to prosper financially. The preachers, alongside their followers, are quick to come up with justifications for their actions. The Lord gives power to get **wealth** (Deuteronomy 8:18). If that is not convincing, they tell you, The blessing of the Lord makes **rich**, and it adds no sorrow. If that is still not convincing, The Lord will supply **all your needs** according to **his riches** in glory through Christ. And to clear all doubts, **Beloved,** concerning **all things I pray you to prosper and to be in health** just as your soul prospers. It is evident that it is God's will for you believers to be wealthy, after all, for your sakes He became poor, that through His poverty **you might become rich**.

For this cause, you pray continuously for wealth, and equate the blessings of God strictly to mean financial wealth. Can the rich make it into God's coming kingdom? Yes. Is it very easy? No. For many, their money is their god. It is what you wake up to think about. It is the idol you have set up in your heart. It is what you put your trust in. You want to acquire as much as you can, and contentment is never an option. Your shepherds make it worse making you think that the one who is poor is cursed or sinful. Only if you knew how difficult it is for the rich to enter into God's kingdom.

Your pastors have shown you from the Scriptures as justification for the gospel of prosperity which they preach to you, but they are deceived. They cherry pick quotations from the Scriptures to suit their claims even though, the focus in those passages was not really financial wealth. They tell you the law is no more and Christ has come to 'abolish' it, so you don't have to keep the commandments and the laws, yet, they ask you to turn the pages of your guide to Deuteronomy 28 to claim the blessings there. Are these blessings not for faithfully keeping the law? If the law is abolished as you claim, should the blessings not with it? You are quick to pick a part of the first five books which have blessings pronounced, but you say, Christ did away with the law. You be your own judge. An opportunist seeks self glory and satisfaction at zero cost. If you know to claim the blessings attached with keeping the Sabbath and obeying God's commandments, surely the curses be upon you if you fail to keep them. If the law is done away with, so should the blessings and the curses. But you claim the law is done away with and so are the curses, but the blessings of it stands till this day. How faulty is your reasoning? If you claim the blessings for obedience to the law, surely, the curses for disobedience be upon you.

The Lord sure gives the power to get wealth, but you skip right over the obvious part where it says to **remember the Lord your God.** This verse tells us that our strength, and all that we achieve (including one's wealth), are done only by the help of God. It is not by might nor by your mental prowess, and so, all the glory must be to Him. Your preachers pick out this part without mentioning one which is even more important. Go a step down and read the conclusion of the statement; "should you **at all forget the Lord your God, and walk after other gods, to serve and to worship them, I testify against you that you shall surely perish. As the nations which the Lord destroys before you, so shall you perish, because you have been disobedient to the voice of the Lord your God**. The understanding is very clear. Remember the Lord and obey His voice because He accomplishes all things for you; but if you do not, doom is decreed. But your preachers pick this one line to back up their claims disregarding completely the message in this section.

Again, the blessing of the Lord makes one rich, and **He adds no sorrow with it.** It is not until you pray your way to it that God gives you wealth. It says, the blessing of the Lord. Where does the blessing come from? The blessing comes as a result of faithfully obeying the voice of the Lord. This is a reiteration of the aforementioned verse. If you do right, and carefully obey the commandments of the Lord, the blessing is yours. When you check a section (Deuteronomy 28) to see the blessing pronounced upon the faithful ones, you have an understanding what Proverbs 10:22 says. You understand the message it passes across. If you keep God's commandments, you are blessed. Just like Abraham was, this blessing as in Deuteronomy 28:3-13) makes you rich even without you making any serious efforts or going through pains and struggles. When your prayers make you rich, you will have to pray continuously or rely on the money when unpleasant events like the invasion of a plague happens. But if the Lord's blessing has caused you to be rich, it adds no sorrow, no pain, no sickness, no accident. It is peace all around because your way pleases God. You will not have to spend minutes or hours specially praying for wealth, it comes as a reward for your obedience. You tend to pray for wealth because you do not faithfully keep the commandments of the Lord. Thus, you pray to get it. Besides, why do you have to pray for it? Is that why you serve the Lord? If the wealth is not promised, would you rather serve another who would promise you wealth?

The Lord will **supply all your NEEDS.** Very clearly stated. If wealth was a necessity, only the wealthy would live well above four score years. On the contrary, some who are rich die before the poor do. Have I said wealth is evil and undesirable? No. But the love of money is the root of all evil and the bedrock of destruction. Many of your desires are wants. They are possessions which could cause you to forget the Lord as God warns in Deuteronomy 8, but all you care about is the satisfaction of your flesh, and in your delusion you say, "if you will make me wealthy, I will serve you with my substance. I will be even more faithful." You think it is service to God when you pay your tithes and offerings? How about the state of your heart and the one who rules it? God or money? Let no one deceive you. God will surely supply all your needs, but you should not confuse your needs with your wants.

Beloved, concerning all things I pray you to prosper and to be in health, **even as your soul prospers.** Here is how you tell between an individual whose treasure and desires are for this temporal world with little or no true focus on the eternal one from an individual whose complete focus and thoughts are on things above. The one whose focus is on the things of this world picks a message of financial prosperity from this verse. Whereas, the one whose focus is on things above picks from this same verse a spiritual message of the prosperity of one's soul. Why should your flesh prosper at the detriment of your soul? Did John not say clearly that you prosper and be in health **even as** your soul prospers? But your end-time preachers overlook the importance of these highlighted words, focusing on the comfort of your flesh. John says, prosper as your soul prospers. While you journey on earth, may your soul prosper, and as your soul prospers so may you and in good health. A prosperous soul is one who is having a successful journey on the earth. A successful journey on the earth is one moving unbothered on the narrow way. If your ways do not please God, your soul is impoverished. But since many are led by sight, and they like to measure one's success by how much money or possession a mortal has got, emphasis is placed on physical and financial prosperity. Many are very rich and comfortable physically, but their soul is very poor and nearly in a hopeless state. Have you read the message to the messenger of the church? I know your works, that you are neither cold nor hot; but I would that you were cold or hot. Because you are lukewarm and neither cold nor hot, I will vomit you out of My mouth. For you say, I am (physically) rich and have grown rich, and I have need of nothing but you do not realize that you are (spiritually) wretched and poor, and miserable, and blind, and naked. I counsel you to buy from Me gold which has been refined by fire (The Holy Spirit) so that you (your soul) may be rich and white garment (purity) so that you may be clothed and the shame of your nakedness hidden, and eye-salve to anoint your spiritual eyes so that you may see the deception. Maybe your preacher places more emphasis on your comfort and financial stability in this present world and he makes you pray unceasingly until you are wealthy, of more importance is the state of your soul to God. Is it prosperous or impoverished?

For your sakes Christ became poor, that through His poverty you might become rich. Christ mentioned that the poor in spirit are blessed because theirs is God's kingdom. He suffered that much persecution and eventually His life as a ransom for your soul so that you should not save your soul with your life. He endured the cross that you may have free and unrestricted access to the Father through His sacrifice. But if you are so led by the flesh that you cannot read this message from the quote but your flesh refuses to pick out any other message other than financial prosperity, then, check out what Paul's message focused on. You pick out a line of the numerous words and wrongly use it to justify the claims of your own flesh. Has Paul said Christ was financially poor so that you can live comfortably and in financial stability? Was that the actual message in that section? Paul was going to address a key activity central to this journey; sharing one's possession among the needy brethren, he started off with a reminder that their wealth is given by God. And so, this should be extended to ensure equality. God has blessed you so that the brethren would not suffer. But what do we have at this time? Though a fraction of the congregation have been blessed financially, they have no regard for the ones suffering among them. They would rather compete among themselves for the best choice of dress or the best cars. They would rather give to the world that they may get praise and recognition. They would rather increase the amount of the tithes and offerings which they give than help a brother who suffers. If you have a thousand, yet there is one among you who suffers, you should bow your head in shame. If you had millions yet, in your congregation, there are those who are suffering, God will ask you what you have done with your wealth. You have taken after the world who make for themselves class. They love to move with people who are in their social rank, looking down on the poor. Has Christ taught us this way?

Your preachers like to go into these parts of the Scriptures frequently, but seldom or never lead you to the part which says, **he who covers his sins will not prosper.** Despite the increasing rate of immoralities among you, and the widespread abomination, they continue to preach about the comfort and prosperity of your flesh at the expense of your soul. Though many sexually immoral, cheaters, and liars are among you, they continue to step up in your podium, and you think God is present because you feel something. God's judgement will come upon the wicked. Your sins will be exposed, and your shame revealed to the whole world.

Trust in God.

The days of evil approach, and how shall a man endure except he has an absolute trust in God? The common problem is, many think it is the words which state the fact when it is actually one's actions. They ask to scream if you love God, and you scream. Within you is a feeling of satisfaction after the noise, and you are absolutely convinced you love God— just because your lying tongue said so. But the works of your hands and the activities of your flesh evidently scream hatred towards God and love for the world. Questioning your trust in God should not be a polar question where you either say yes or no. Ask anyone, and they would say they do trust God. But do they, really? Do you really trust God?

The trust of some is in their money. They are not unsettled by sickness because they are confident the healer would get it resolved once they get to the clinic with their money. The love of money would even significantly reduce the time an individual spend before God. Some put their trust in men, some in their possession, some in their knowledge.

When you trust God, you do not have a fallback plan. For instance, if you got ill, you would immediately visit the clinic, right? But then, if you got ill, could you confidently say, "I know the God I serve would heal me. If He does not, fine, but my salvation will not come from the devil". In order words, can you say, "I trust God to save me, but if I die along the line then, I die." Did the three Hebrews not do this?

It is not trust when you have tried certain means, and then turn to God after it failed. It is not trust when you approach God first, and at the same time, you are making up a second plan in case God does not heed. It is not trust when you are more focused on saving your life than you are on going with God's will. It is not trust in God when you say, "if you truly exist, then you have to do this." The three knew God could save them, yet, if He chose not to they were not going to lose faith. Abraham knew he could die, yet he left his comfort for a land he had not been shown. Daniel was not afraid of the lions, neither was he praying so hard for his enemies to be consumed. He did not think God was obligated to save him also. For him, if he died, it mattered not. This is trust. Trust is when you place your life in the hands of another.

What do you call trust these days? If you really placed your life in God's hands, you would rather choose death than go to the devil for help. You would rather have only one plan and faithfully wait for God's will even if it requires your life. You learn to trust God only when He is the only option available to you. Have you placed your life in God's hands? Would you faithfully wait on God's plan even if your life is on the line? Do you really trust God or you are consistently trying to save your own life?

God answers prayers at a certain location

If they say to you, Behold He is in the desert, do not go. Behold He is in the secret chambers, do not believe it. For many, there shepherds deceive them saying, you are believers. But, they are not, they are only seekers of miracles. Therefore, they travel from mountain to valley, from the north to the south seeking wonders. The one who performs wonders in their sight then is deemed God sent and they wander after him. Like those in Samaria, these continue to deceive them claiming to be of God when they are wolves in sheep's clothing.

Your shepherds call for prayers in a certain location, and in your heart you believe your prayer would be answered only if you are in that location at that time. Is your god limited by time and space? Is the Lord a God at hand, and not a God afar off? But because you do not truly believe, you have tied your faith to their erroneous claim of God answering your prayers faster in a certain location.

The One I serve is everywhere and every time, and, as long as you do right, He will grant your requests which are not contradictory to His plans for you. God does not reside in a place, He resides in you. If God resides in you then, He is everywhere you go. Whether you be in the desert or in the cave, or on a journey, or in your home, He is right there, because He is with you and is indwelling within you. But when you do not know the true God and your faith in Him is not full, you will be made to think that God will answer your requests at a certain location, but when you choose to be in another location there is less chance of your requests being granted. The One whom I serve does not work this way.

Doom is pronounced unto the shepherds who destroy and scatter the sheep of His pasture. He has appointed you to feed His flock, yet you have driven them away from His presence and led them into the world. Behold, as surely as the Lord lives, He will bring upon you the evil of your wrongdoings. As you have defiled and spoiled the house of God, so shall God defile and spoil you and your household.

The earth is covered in adultery, and even your leaders join in committing this abomination, you cover your sins by calling on the name of the Lord, and you continually live in wickedness; according to the dictate of your heart. Now, this is the word of the Lord, because you have done this, I will bring upon you evil in the year that I visit you. For you have prophesied lies and have caused the people of God to fall into error.

Listen not to them who by their name prophesy yet claim to prophesy in God's name. They tell false dreams and comfort in lies. They stand in your synagogue saying, The Lord has said. They tell you they have received a vision from the Lord, yet, I never knew these ones neither have I given them My words to speak. They comfort you in lies and speak peace and prosperity, yet, they speak of their own heart and desires. The evil to come shall be sudden, one no man will have a prior knowledge of its coming, and by this you shall know that the mouth of the Lord has spoken this.

The anger of the Lord is against those who falsely call on His name. It shall not return until He has done what He intends to do. Has He not by the mouth of the elect spoken it, that judgement should begin in the house of God? Therefore, God has set His sword against those who tell false prophecies

and false dreams; for their shame shall be eternal
and their reward fully paid.

Other Works

Evidence of Holy Spirit's Presence; Gifts or Fruit?

First Love: God's definition of True Love.

Be holy, for I am Holy.

Power

The Ten Virgins; Wise or Foolish?

Praise